Why Living Things Need...

Homes

Daniel Nunn

Heinemann Library
Chicago, Illinois

www.capstonepub.com
Visit our website to find out
more information about
Heinemann-Raintree books.

To order:
☎ Phone 800-747-4992
🖥 Visit www.capstonepub.com
   to browse our catalog and order online.

Edited by Dan Nunn, Rebecca Rissman, and Sian Smith
Designed by Joanna Hinton-Malivoire
Picture research by Ruth Blair
Production by Victoria Fitzgerald
Originated by Capstone Global Library Ltd
Printed in the United States of America in Eau Claire,
Wisconsin. 072018   000789

15 14 13
10 9 8 7 6 5 4 3 2

Library of Congress Cataloging-in-Publication Data
Nunn, Daniel.
  Homes / Daniel Nunn.
    p. cm.—(Why living things need)
  Includes bibliographical references and index.
  ISBN 978-1-4329-5915-9 (hc)—ISBN 978-1-4329-5921-0
(pb) 1. Dwellings—Juvenile literature. 2. Housing—Juvenile
literature. 3. Animal housing—Juvenile literature. I. Title.
  TH4811.5.N86 2012
  591.56'4—dc23   2011014649

Acknowledgments
We would like to thank the following for permission to
reproduce photographs: Corbis pp.10 (© Lance Nelson/
Stock Photos), 11 (© Juice Images), 17 (© D. Robert & Lorri
Franz); Photolibrary pp.7 (Michael Krabs/Imagebroker), 8
(Eric Baccega/Age fotostock), 12 (Fritz Polking/Peter Arnold
Images), 20 (J-L. Klein & M-L. Hubert/Bios); Shutterstock pp.4
(© Gerald A. DeBoer), 5 (© dusan964), 5 (© Rob Marmion),
5 (© Kevin E. Beasley), 5 (© tomy), 6 (© Tony Campbell), 9
(© tfrisch99), 13 (© Noam Armonn), 14 (© Caitlin Mirra),
15 (© Groomee), 16 (© John Carnemolla), 18 (© Arno
van Dulmen), 19 (© Vishnevskiy Vasily), 21 (© Monkey
Business Images), 22 (© visceralimage), 22 (© jokter), 22 (©
Inhabitant), 23 (© Tony Campbell), 23 (© Vishnevskiy Vasily).

Front cover photograph of a puffin reproduced with
permission of Photolibrary (Fritz Polking/Peter Arnold
Images). Back cover photograph of a bird building a nest
reproduced with permission of Shutterstock (© tfrisch99).

We would like to thank Nancy Harris, Dee Reid, and Diana
Bentley for their assistance in the preparation of this book.

Every effort has been made to contact copyright holders of
any material reproduced in this book. Any omissions will
be rectified in subsequent printings if notice is given to
the publisher.

Contents

What Is a Home?

beehive

bees

A home is a place where something lives.

There are different kinds of homes.

Living Things and Homes

People and other animals are
living things.

Living things need homes.

Some animals find homes.

This bear lives in a cave.

Some animals build homes.

This bird lives in a nest.

Some people build homes, too.

This person lives on a boat.

Why Do Living Things Need Homes?

Homes keep living things safe.

Homes keep living things safe from the weather.

Homes keep animals safe from other animals.

Homes keep animals warm and dry.

How Do Living Things Use Homes?

Some living things sleep in their homes.

Foxes sleep in their homes.

Some living things eat in their homes.

Birds bring food to their nests.

Some living things care for their young in their homes.

People care for their young
in their homes.

Homes Quiz

Which of these things does not need a home?

Answer on page 24

Picture glossary

living thing something that is alive, such as an animal or a plant

nest home made by birds or other animals out of grass or twigs

Index

Answer to question on page 22
The pig and the eagle need homes.
The traffic light does not need a home.

Notes for parents and teachers

Before reading

Talk about why people live in homes. For example, homes keep people warm and dry, homes give people a place to sleep, a place to eat their food, and somewhere to keep their belongings. Ask them if they can think of some homes that animals have. What does a bird make its home out of? Where do bees make their home? Where do rabbits make their homes?

After reading

• Demonstrate how to use an information book to discover some interesting facts about animal homes. Take one example of an animal home and draw a simple sketch of the home on paper. Add a caption and talk about the writing process as you write. Invite children to draw different homes, for example, a cave, a nest, a rabbit's burrow, or a fox's den. Help them to add simple captions, for example: A fox's home is called a den.

• Tell the children they are going to pretend to be different animals looking for their homes. For example, explain that they are going to be rabbits. They should bunny hop around until you say that they have found their home. Then they can pretend to crawl down the burrow and lie down to sleep. Repeat with ideas for an owl in its hole, a bee in its hive, a bear in its cave, a spider in its web, and a horse in its stable.